In clear, precise prose, Dr. Laurie Weiss makes the case for Logosynthesis, a tool for releasing psychic energy long bound up in stressful experiences. With strong supporting anecdotes, she introduces the reader to a deceptively simple method for enriching one's life. Fascinating.

– Mike Keefe,
Pulitzer Prize-Winning cartoonist (US)

You have an absolute GEM In this sweet little book! I love it. I could not wait to use it! It is simple, to the point and makes the reader comfortable with using it.

– Rhondda Hartman, R.N., M.A. Author,
Natural Childbirth Exercises (US)

I am struck by the clarity of your writing and the straightforward way you have organized and presented the material. I very much liked the step-by-step instruction! Your personal anecdotes made your own experience with Logo-synthesis more present and accessible. I am sure it will make a meaningful difference in the lives of many people. Bravo!

– Foster Brashear, Designer,
Electronic Systems and Devices (US)

You have a very engaging writing style easy to read. Great case examples. THIS BOOK IS GOING TO BE A VERY IMPORTANT TOOL FOR SELF-COACHING. Many, many thanks.

– Julie Jacinthe Arsenault, MSW Clinical Social Worker, Psychotherapist, Logosynthesis Practitioner (Canada)

This book opens doors to stuck emotional spaces we experience, regardless of "who," "where," "how," or "why" we are. It was, for me, an empowering read. I predict this book (and Logosynthesis) to be beneficial to individuals, families, and faith groups. The "sentences" proposed, are liberating and truly help me look at life challenges from an "energy viewpoint." I agree with Dr. Weiss's own words, that this book and its approach is a great resource for "spiritual awakening and transformation."

– Ralph Datema, D.Min., M.Div., LMFT, Diplomate – American Association of Pastoral Counselors (US)

Your book explains the Logosynthesis process in a way that will make it easy for me to use this process to relieve stress and fear from various incidences in my past and help me release the energy that I have given up to them. I don't know how or why it works, I just have experienced the relief it brings.

– Karen Bartholow, Home Health Care Provider (US)

I work primarily with corporate coaching clients and executives and it is amazing how I end up using Logosynthesis with the majority of them. I am thrilled that you've written this as a simple guide which they can refer to and use for themselves. Thank you for doing this.

– Pamela Burkhalter, Management Consultant, Facilitator, Logosynthesis Practitioner (Switzerland)

What a wonderful and inspiring book. Your writing is easily understood, in spite of the very complicated subject matter you are dealing with. If everyone knew and used this tool, everyday life would greatly improve for most of us. I can't imagine anyone who would not benefit from making it a part of daily practice.

– Judy Warren, M.ED., Educator (US)

I like it a lot. I was drawn into the story lines that you cleverly presented and especially like how you interweave your personal experiences. Examples are clear, interesting and easy to understand and relate to.

– Trish North, Director, Logosynthesis Canada;
Logosynthesis Practitioner (Canada)

You have a wonderful way of putting things into clear words and digestible form.

– Karin Martin (Frischluft) Business Consultant, Coach, Logosynthesis Practitioner (Switzerland)

Letting it GO

RELIEVE ANXIETY AND TOXIC STRESS IN JUST A FEW MINUTES USING ONLY WORDS

DR. LAURIE WEISS

Empowerment Systems Books

Letting it Go

Relieve Anxiety and Toxic Stress in
Just a Few Minutes Using Only Words

Laurie Weiss, Ph.D

ISBN 978-0-9743113-5-7 (paper)
ISBN 978-0-9743113-6-4 (ebook)

Publisher's Cataloging-In-Publication Data

(Prepared by The Donohue Group, Inc.)

Names: Weiss, Laurie, 1939-

Title: Letting it go: relieve anxiety and toxic stress in just a
few minutes using only words / Dr. Laurie Weiss.

Description: Littleton, CO: Empowerment Systems Books, [2016] |
"Rapid relief with Logosynthesis®." | Includes bibliographical references.

Identifiers: ISBN 978-0-9743113-5-7 | ISBN 978-0-9743113-6-4 (ebook)

Subjects: LCSH: Stress management. | Self-talk. | Affirmations. | Anxiety.

Classification: LCC BF575.S75 W45 2016 (print) |LCC BF575.S75 (ebook) |
DDC 155.9/042--dc23

Published By:

Empowerment Systems Books

506 West Davies Way

Littleton, CO 80120 USA

Phone 303.794.5379

LaurieWeiss@EmpowermentSystems.com

www.EmpowermentSystems.com

Logosynthesis® is a registered trademark,
owned by Willem Lammers in Maienfeld, Switzerland.

Limits of Liability / Disclaimer of Warranty:

EXTRA GIFT

Once you finish reading this book
be sure to claim your gift.
Quick Start Guide:
Using Logosynthesis to Release
Anxiety, Stress and Worry
www.BooksbyLaurie.com/guide

ALSO BY LAURIE WEISS

Stop These Common Beliefs from Poisoning Your Marriage: A Conversation with Experts (The Secrets of Happy Relationships Series) (with Jonathan B. Weiss)

99 Things Women Wish They Knew Before Saying 'I Do:' Your Guide to a Satisfying and Fulfilling Marriage

Being Happy Together: How to Have a Fabulous Relationship with Your Life Partner in Less Than an Hour a Week

What Is The Emperor Wearing? Truth-telling In Business Relationships

Emotional Self-Help: I Don't Need Therapy, But...Where Do I Turn For Answers?

An Action Plan for Your Inner Child: Parenting Each Other

Recovery from Co-Dependency: It's Never Too Late to Reclaim Your Childhood (with Jonathan B. Weiss)

124 Tips for Having a Great Relationship

Dare To Say It: How to Have Important Conversations that Build Working Relationships

Doesn't Anyone Else See This? It's Hard To Tell the Truth When the Truth Is Bad News (The Speak Your Mind Series)

How to Marry Mr. Right: Avoid Making a Big Mistake (The Secrets of Happy Relationships Series)

Save Your Marriage: Avoid Divorce and Feel Loved and Connected Again (The Secrets of Happy Relationships Series)

PREFACE

Introducing Dr. Willem Lammers

In this book, you'll learn how a new and highly effective method of guided self-change can help relieve your toxic stress and anxiety. This methodology was discovered by Dr. Willem Lammers and is becoming increasingly popular in Europe and spreading to other parts of the world.

I am very honored that Dr. Lammers is offering this preface to my work.

Laurie Weiss, Ph.D.

* * *

If you can't make it simple, you don't understand it well enough.

– Albert Einstein

The method presented in this book is the result of 40+ years of experience in the guidance of people on their life path. In these years I studied many approaches to coaching, counseling and psychotherapy, but again and again I came to the conclusion that there must be something more simple, more elegant, more effective. Coming of age as a professional in the sixties, I learned Transactional Analysis, Psychoanalysis, hypnotherapy, NLP, EMDR and many of the new models of energy psychology.

Between 2001 and 2005 I went through a crisis in my motivation and creativity as a professional: I was still convinced that there must be a more direct way to guide people through their pain, into their development. I also knew this way wouldn't be rooted in more concepts, more neurology and more techniques, but in a deeper understanding of human beings.

Human beings are more than biological machines with a wet computer between their ears. In reality, we are energetic manifestations of something bigger, wider and higher, which I call Essence, and this Essence is the answer to the question why we live here on earth. If we lose the connection to what we really are, we become the slaves of our biological and psychological needs, and if these needs are not fulfilled we're caught in fear, guilt, grief and greed.

From the increasing awareness that we are more than our physical body and our mind I discovered Logosynthesis in 2005, and I have spent my years since then to make it simple. First as a model for my colleagues in the healing professions, then as a method people could use for themselves to cope with the challenges of daily life.

Laurie Weiss, whom I deeply respect as a colleague, as an author and as a fellow human being, has taken the simplicity, elegance and effectiveness of Logosynthesis for self-coaching to new heights. Her use of examples from years of practice, her clear style of writing, her deep understanding of the theory and the method of Logosynthesis, all wrapped in a deeply human attitude are guaranteed to open your eyes and your heart to a new future for yourself and those who you love.

That doesn't mean that you have to solve every problem on your own. Our growing international community of Logosynthesis Practitioners is here to assist you on your path to healing, your path to discovering who you are and why you're here.

Maienfeld, Switzerland, January 2016
Dr. Willem Lammers
Founder and developer of Logosynthesis

CONTENTS

CHAPTER ONE

DISSOLVING TOXIC STRESS

There cannot be a stressful crisis next week. My schedule is already full.

– Henry Kissinger

Are you singing the song you came here to sing?

– Lawrence LeShan, Joe Sabah

You want to live with less stress and more joy. You just want to stop feeling so anxious about all the things you think you should be handling when you already feel like a stretched rubber band. You wonder what happened to all the energy you used to have.

But, no matter how hard you try to stay in control, stuff keeps happening. People make demands on you and you expect yourself to be able to do it all, so of course, you're stressed.

- Then you can't stop thinking about it all.

- You start feeling anxious and it drains your energy.

- You know you should let it go but you can't figure out how.

- You try to fix it, but take out your frustration in ways that make things worse.

And furthermore, you don't have time or resources to get it fixed!

You are not alone! In the 45 years I have been helping people heal their lives I have used many different tools to help them calm their anxiety, take charge of their busy lives and find what they need to live joyfully. And I have used those tools on myself as well.

So imagine my surprise when a long-time colleague and friend showed me a new tool that simply blew me away!

I Was Amazed

It happened this way. My husband and I went to dinner with old friends after a day at a professional conference in Montreal. Our friends picked a Mexican restaurant which was supposed to be quiet and pleasant. We live in Colorado and can get that kind of food any time but it was a special treat for them.

I am a "highly sensitive person" whose body rejects highly spiced food and loud noises and the evening did not go well. Waiters kept promising food I could eat and delivering food that made my mouth burn and induced violent coughing. As we sat there very loud families arrived and the mariachis began to play trumpets! Can you imagine how stressed I felt?

I excused myself while my husband paid the bill and went outside into a beautiful quiet evening to calm myself down. I did some breathing exercises and tapping and I thought I was fine. Then the friend came out and asked if I was OK. I told him, truthfully, that I was. He asked me to describe what happened and I did my best to explain how my body had become extremely tense.

He asked if I would try something new and had me repeat some words I barely understood. Suddenly I experienced a whole new level of deep relaxation of the remaining tension that I had not even been aware of before. I was stunned! I asked what he had done and he told me he had used a new European technique called Logosynthesis.

That happened in 2010. I started taking professional Logosynthesis training a few months later and it has not only changed the way I practice coaching and psychotherapy, allowing me to help my clients much more rapidly and with much less pain, it has changed my own life.

One change is that since that encounter in 2010, my life-long stress reaction to noise has simply disappeared. Another change is that after my first training weekend, which I had been reluctant to schedule because of my stress reaction to the intense overstimulation of airplane travel, I traveled home and simply forgot to be stressed. I have been able to travel on airplanes without any particular reaction ever since. Sadly, I still can't manage spicy food.

After several years of study and supervision my husband and I have become the first and (as of this writing) only certified Practitioners and Basic Trainers of Logosynthesis in the United States.

Logo What?

Dr. Willem Lammers, DPSYCH, MSC, TSTA, the Swiss-Dutch discoverer of Logosynthesis and author of several important books on the subject, has asked me to create a simple, more accessible version of this information for people who are looking for help managing stress, anxiety and myriad other challenges in their lives.

On the surface, Logosynthesis is a surprisingly simple tool. You learn to notice certain things about yourself and the flow of your life energy. When you find something that is uncomfortable or out of alignment you say three sentences and notice your own responses to each sentence.

Sometimes you don't notice anything at all. Sometimes old memories are activated. Sometimes you feel weird, surprising physical sensations. Often your experience of discomfort shifts and whatever was causing you distress vanishes.

The premises on which Logosynthesis are based are also simple. I will explain them in more detail later but this is enough to get started.

If you have any type of spiritual or religious practice you probably already recognize that at your core you have a true Self or Essence. When you live your life as your true Self you experience a flowing energy often labeled as joy.

When your energy is not flowing this way you may experience various kinds of discomfort. Life is messy and you frequently encounter all kinds of stress that block the free flow of your energy.

Willem Lammers says that energy is either moving or stuck and that it is in the right place or the wrong place. The purpose of this process is to get energy that is stuck moving again and to move energy from the wrong place to the right place.

The first time I heard about this process, I simply dismissed it. My friends had tried to share it with me before our evening at the restaurant and I just didn't get it. So rather than tell you about the process, let me share a few more stories about my experience using it.

An Experiment That Worked

The first time we (my husband Jonathan and myself) explained what we had experienced to a group of friends they wanted a demonstration. A 60-something-year-old woman volunteered, explaining that for as long as she could remember she felt scared and noticeably flinched back when a car in which she was a front seat passenger approached another car. Her husband verified this behavior happened nearly every time they were in the car together.

Her energy was clearly stuck in something but we were not sure what so we asked her to repeat sentences focusing on "this experience of flinching back." After each sentence we asked her to notice what she experienced and she reported a memory of being in an accident where her head had hit the windshield of a car when she was 17 years old.

We had her say the sentences again focusing on "this memory of hitting the windshield" and she reported feeling relaxed. Then, because we had been told that sometimes personal energy gets stuck in objects, we asked her to say the sentences focusing on taking her stuck energy back from the windshield and she reported even more relaxation. The entire process took about 15 minutes.

Several weeks later we were astonished when she reported that she had not flinched even once since we had done the process. Her husband agreed.

Many months later he wrote a letter saying that the change seemed to be permanent. You can see the letter at LogosynthesisColorado.com. Magic???

Magic or not, there was something very different about this tool. The more I experimented with it, the more excited I became. I was able to help clients resolve painful issues with so little fuss that they often forgot the reason for their newfound freedom. I found that work that used to take many months could now be resolved in just a few weekly sessions.

Yes, I will tell you the magic words, but not yet. You need more information about choosing your focus points before knowing the exact wording of the sentences that will be useful to you. Even after you learn those sentences, I suggest reading this book through the instructions in chapter 7 before experimenting with using them yourself.

Giving Up Suffering

Then there was the work I was able to do by myself! I've known for years that "suffering is optional," which means that we don't need to focus on existing discomfort and tell ourselves stories that make us even more uncomfortable. However, I never expected my license to suffer to be revoked. Once I learned how to use Logosynthesis to release my own anxious feelings I simply could not justify letting them continue to bother me.

It usually works this way for me. When I am preparing for bed the unresolved stuff of the day tends to surface. One evening while brushing my teeth I kept going over and over the ways I could have responded differently to a fairly nasty conversation with a man I barely knew. Since it was over and unlikely to cause any further problems (other than those I created myself) in my life, I decided it would be nice to stop thinking about it now instead of lying awake and obsessing about it later.

This would have been easy to say but hard to do without my new tool. I used the sentences focused on the belief that I should have acted differently. Suddenly I had a very clear picture of myself at 10 years old in a new school being teased by a girl named Betty. Now we would call that teasing bullying but that concept for teasing was unknown 65 years ago.

The kind of vivid picture I remembered contains an amazing amount of information: the things we remember as well as all the other things that are present but out of our immediate consciousness. That kind of picture creates a powerful focal point for this work.

I used the sentences again (aloud, but garbled, I was brushing my teeth) focused on this memory. I found that my worrying about what I could have, would have, should have said earlier in the day completely disappeared. I was relaxed and went to sleep.

You Can Learn To Do This

I have created this book to give you enough information for you to use this tool yourself just as I did. As you develop your skill you will be able to use it when you are feeling stuck, stressed, anxious, overwhelmed, depressed, or otherwise upset. It will help you to relieve your distress, reclaim your energy and get on with your life.

You'll also learn when it would probably be a better choice for you to ask a professional therapist or coach to help you resolve these issues. You will find a list of helpful resources at the end of the book.

CHAPTER TWO

IS SUFFERING REALLY OPTIONAL?

This instant is the only time there is.

– Course in Miracles

The reason for most of your distress is often very different than you think it is. Remember the two examples in the last chapter. My friend seemed to be reacting to approaching another car when she was a passenger but the real cause of her reaction was the trauma that had occurred many years earlier.

The reason I was obsessing about my minor unsuccessful conversation was not the encounter itself. I was really reacting to being bullied over a half century ago and some of my energy was still stuck in my past.

Energy Gets Stuck

You may think it is normal and unavoidable to feel stressed out or hurt or anxious about various situations in your life. When you examine those things you discover that they have already happened or you believe they will happen sometime in the future. Most people you encounter probably agree that those reactions are just a necessary part of living. And the stress and drama are certainly major elements of the stories we love to watch in the media.

The truth is that most of this suffering is completely unnecessary. Sadly, it is hard to opt out of this pervasive cultural belief system. It's hard to even imagine what life would be like without all this drama. Part of the reason for this is almost everyone believes that the distress they experience as adults is caused by the various challenges they encounter in their daily lives.

Another way of looking at the situation is that if we had all of our life energy available to us, we could easily manage most uncomfortable situations. Then the challenge becomes locating and reclaiming our life energy that has somehow been misplaced during the course of our lives.

Over-Reacting Means Energy is Stuck

Sometimes you respond to challenges and forget they were stressful; the ones you over-react to are the problem.

My friend and I both over-reacted to minor stress—stressful situations that most people would simply respond to and forget about. We each got stuck in our own past life experiences. We each had forgotten about the old situations but our energy about those incomplete experiences and our emotions associated with them held us in the past instead of letting us solve problems in the present moment and forget about them.

Can you tell when you are over-reacting? Over-reacting is a good signal that you are reacting to something else. Signals that you are over-reacting include:

- You just can't stop thinking about something. You keep trying to think about something else but you always come back to rethinking the same situation over and over again.

- You always get upset (angry, teary, worried) when you are reminded about someone, someplace, or some event, even if it happened a long time ago.

- Anniversaries or other reminders of difficult experiences are difficult for you.

- You get physically uncomfortable (butter-flies, tension headaches, pounding heart) when you need to talk to someone—often an authority figure.

- You get your feelings hurt easily.

- You have an intense reaction (anger, sadness, fear) because of something someone else says or does.

- You feel very judgmental in response to certain ordinary situations like traffic or others making mistakes.

These over-reactions are examples of your life energy being stuck.

When you were born your life energy was freely available and you used it to attach to your parents as all babies do. But as things happen you lose bits of it by using it to try to protect yourself when you react to problems. This happens to everyone because no one had perfect parents or grew up in a perfectly responsive environment.

These problems overwhelm you because you don't have enough resources to manage them when they occur. That may be because you are a child and simply lack the maturity that comes with growing up—or you may have experienced a truly traumatic situation. In any case you need that energy back for other things now, but you usually don't even realize that you left it somewhere in your past.

Letting Go Isn't Easy

Life is all about attachment and letting go. We need attachment for survival and we need to let go for growth. You were attached to your mother with your umbilical cord and being born broke that attachment and allowed you to join the world as a separate being. Then your first and most critical task is to reattach in a new way.

Once you attached, you had to learn to let go. That is a hard lesson. When you learned to hold on to something—like a piece of furniture—you did not know how to open your hand and let go. So you stayed in one place and when you got tired you probably screamed until somebody came along and released your fingers. You probably then promptly pulled yourself up again and went through the same routine until you finally learned to let go.

This dilemma is repeated in all sorts of situations. Holding on to familiar people, situations, and beliefs feels safe and you are torn between trying to hold on and your natural urge to grow and let go. It's tricky under the best of circumstances, and since those can't always be available, every one of us runs into problems we just can't solve by ourselves—and it is painful and scary for us. So instead of solving the problems, we use our energy to protect ourselves from the pain.

When you do this it is almost like surrounding your perception of this painful situation with your energy and freezing it there to make sure it won't trouble you any longer. You carry these frozen bits of encapsulated pain everywhere you go. My work with Logosynthesis has convinced me that these frozen bits actually exist in the personal space that surrounds you.

Everyone's Energy Gets Stuck Sometimes

Here is one way life energy gets stuck when you encounter something that is too much for you to manage and integrate using the resources you have on hand. You can easily imagine a baby or small child being overwhelmed by a new situation. Problems occur all the time, even in the most loving and attentive families.

Imagine that Mom is exhausted and taking a nap, thinking that her child is asleep. She doesn't realize that her toddler is learning to climb out of his crib. He manages to get out, open a closed door and slip out of the house. He can't get back in. He whimpers for help but she can't hear him and only finds him an hour later in the back yard after a frantic search. They are both traumatized and a little bit of their life energy gets stuck in the situation.

Of course, in a family where things are not going so well and a parent is ill or suffering from an addiction or even distracted by way too many responsibilities, a child can get into all kinds of scary and overwhelming situations. Each time that happens, a little more of the child's life energy gets tied up and becomes unavailable to her.

It happens to all of us. As you get older and go to school you're expected to learn to do more and more things. You might have been richly rewarded for being careful not to make any mistakes and decided that being perfect was the only way to survive. Your energy can get so frozen into imagining the terrible consequences of making a mistake that you lose your joy in just trying new things.

Life energy gets stuck when something painful or overwhelming happens that you can't handle. It might have happened 10 minutes or 40 years ago. You freeze it to protect yourself from the pain—perhaps of someone's disapproval. It is like bumping yourself on a table and either holding tight to the bruised spot with your hand or even refusing to go near the table again.

As long as you hold on to the bruised place you can't use your hand for anything else. Twenty or forty years later, if you happen to learn you have not met someone else's expectations you may feel far more ashamed than seems appropriate for the current situation.

When something happens in your daily life that is similar in some way to an event that is frozen in your past, it breaks through your protection and sets off, like a trigger, the distress that is already in place in your life energy system. You just did not even realize your energy was lost in your past—until now.

Today's Distress Connects to Your Stuck Energy

You may not even know that your current problem is a reaction to something that is connected to something else that happened long ago. You just know you feel on edge or worried or can't seem to get around to doing something you want to do. Nevertheless, learning about these triggers and connections may be very important to letting the problem go.

It was for Dennis. He didn't have any idea why he started feeling so anxious about keeping his job. Everything seemed to be going well but he couldn't let go of his feelings of dread or the pounding of his heart each time he entered the building.

If he had come to me for help before I learned to use Logosynthesis, I would have explored what was happening with his supervisor and co-workers and what his hidden fears might be.

If he had gone to his physician for help, he might have been given anti-anxiety medication to help him relax and become dependent on the medication to manage his anxiety for the rest of his life. Fortunately, he was in a workshop where he was learning Logosynthesis as a self-coaching tool.

Logosynthesis Helps You Reclaim Your Energy

Dennis chose to reclaim his energy that was stuck in his pounding heart. When his partner helped him use the sentences the real trigger emerged. It was the new vice-president who reminded him of his deceased father, who had been very critical of mistakes he made when he was a child.

He didn't even report to the vice-president and chances of encountering him on the job were remote. When he used the sentences about all the times his father had criticized him he relaxed. Afterwards, when he imagined having to actually work with the vice-president he felt calm and relaxed. His anxious feelings vanished completely.

The entire process took a lot less than an hour. And it was not even necessary for him to know the original reason for his upset when he started to work. It was just important for him to be open to exploring how his energy got stuck and having the tools to release it.

CHAPTER THREE

YOUR ENERGY IS STUCK

Loving ourselves through the process of owning our story is the bravest thing we'll ever do.

– Brené Brown

Using Logosynthesis, you may not need to go through the entire process of owning your own story, but you will still need courage to explore the signals you send your self; signals that can tell you your vital energy is stuck and unavailable to you.

On a deep level your true Self knows what is good for you. It signals you with tiny messages you so often ignore. It's the little voice inside your head or the way you suddenly relax your shoulders when someone speaks the truth, or the tears behind your eyes when you are deeply touched by an act of kindness.

And yet you don't want to pay attention to those signals. You hold on to the stuck places, even when you know it's not good for you! What happened when you were small and don't remember matters. Energy gets stuck in your cells, your body and your personal space.

You Freeze Energy to Protect Yourself

We need to face stress and learn to manage it in our lives in order to grow up and do our life's work. But it isn't easy and the resources you gather along the way may not be enough at any particular time.

When you can't use the stress you encounter to stimulate your own growth, that stress becomes toxic for you.

That's when you split off parts of yourself and freeze your energy around them because they are too hard to manage. You do this when your experience of your world seems overwhelming. You aren't alone. We all do it.

It does take courage to heed those signals. You froze your energy for a good reason—at least it seemed like a good reason at the time. You froze it to protect yourself from the pain of the stress you did not have the resources to manage and the pain that resulted from your helplessness. Now you may feel a deep sense of dread at the very idea of going into those deeply protected places where your monsters still hide.

Recovering Frozen Energy Can Be Easier Than You Imagine

As a long-time practitioner of psychotherapy, a large part of my job used to be to keep my clients safe while they explored those scary places. When I was just starting to use Logosynthesis in my practice a young woman was referred to me because she had recently revealed a history of sexual abuse to her school counselor. I estimated that her treatment would take about six months.

The abuse had occurred from the time she was five years old until she was eleven. A teenage uncle, part of a large, close, extended family, had been her babysitter and often forced her to engage in inappropriate sexual contact. When I asked why she had not told anyone about the abuse, she said she had kept it secret because telling would have destroyed the family.

I asked if she had an image of what the destroyed family would look like and she had a very vivid image of all the members of the family sitting around a holiday dinner table and shouting angrily at each other. The image was very distressing to her even now, sitting in my office as a 17-year-old high school senior.

In our very first session I asked her to say the Logosynthesis sentences using that image as a target. She reported that the image slowly dissolved and turned into dust, which she swept away. That session ended. A week later she felt much more peaceful and was doing better in school, which was the reason she had originally seen her school counselor.

The next week I asked if she wanted to work with a specific instance of abuse that she remembered vividly. We used the sentences again and that image crumbled to dust as well. We spent the next couple of sessions working on other relatively normal challenges faced by a 17-year-old and then I asked if she wanted to continue working with the sexual abuse problems.

She was thoughtful for a few minutes and then said that nothing she could think of had any emotional charge on it. "It all seems to have gone away." I saw her for a total of 6 sessions in less than 2 months, only focused on the pain of the sexual abuse trauma for a few minutes—long enough to identify the vivid, painful images and the entire problem was resolved!!!

This was an extremely traumatic series of events that she was able to process without needing to re-experience the pain of releasing her frozen energy from all those years and reclaiming her life energy from her past.

Locating Your Frozen Energy is the Challenge

If you have deep, significant trauma from your past that is keeping your life energy stuck, by all means seek professional help to resolve it. For ordinary, everyday frozen energy that resulted from stress in managing your life, using Logosynthesis will require much less courage than you might imagine.

Before you can use the Logosynthesis sentences to reclaim your energy for use in your life now, you need to know where your energy is stuck or frozen. That is why I have not yet told you the exact process.

Once you know where your energy is stuck you will insert a word or phrase that describes your frozen energy into each of three sentences. That is the stuck energy that triggers your distress. We often call it your target. Once you zap your target, you release the energy you used to protect yourself long ago. You also release the energy that was stuck in the original situation, and reclaim it to use now.

What often happens is that before you do the process you feel strong emotions about something in your past every time you think of it. After you do the process the emotional intensity is greatly reduced or disappears completely. You don't necessarily forget what happened, you just don't react to it any longer.

Your biggest challenge in this entire process is discovering where your frozen energy is located. But your frozen energy leaves clues and you can easily follow the trail. You start by noticing what causes you distress in your everyday life.

Clues to Frozen Energy

Here is a list of common ways many people experience distress. They don't necessarily mean your energy is frozen in these spots. They are just suggestions about where to start looking for the hidden energy resources that are either not flowing or stuck in the wrong place.

- Repeatedly forgetting to do something you intend to do.

- Having strong feelings about something that other people don't consider a problem.

- Procrastinating—about anything.

- Having a headache.

- Having some belief you hold about yourself or someone else that doesn't make much sense but you can't seem to let it go.

- Avoiding making a phone call or having a conversation.

- Feeling your stomach churn whenever you think about something.

- Experiencing tightness or tension in some part of your body.

- Feeling stress whenever you think about a particular problem.

- Feeling anxious or scared (they are pretty much the same feeling) and either knowing or not knowing why you feel that way.

When you experience any of these things it often means that just a moment or a millisecond before you experience them you have been reminded in some way of a time when you felt unresourceful or overwhelmed sometime in the past.

You don't need to worry about what reminded you. That can be very subtle like a passing smell, a fragment of a song, seeing a familiar shape—even someone who reminds you of someone who is no longer a part of your life. If you do recognize the trigger, great! If you don't, it does not really matter.

The Answer Can Be Obvious

Here is one situation where someone reclaimed energy without any knowledge of the original problem situation.

I once heard a friend say how scared she felt about some planned, necessary surgery. I imagined that she was frightened about the operation itself or the anesthesia or her recovery time. I asked, "What are you the most scared about?" Her answer surprised me. She was most scared about spending so much money on herself. She did not hesitate to spend similar amounts on other members of her family.

I suggested that she experiment with saying the sentences with the target, "this belief that I don't deserve to spend money on myself." She did. A few days later I asked if she was still scared about spending money on the surgery and she shrugged and said, "It will be whatever it is." She did not even seem to remember how scared she had been. She had the procedure and recovered quickly.

If there was some incident in her past that was connected to spending money on herself, she never explored what it was. She simply recovered the energy frozen into dreading the upcoming operation.

Try This Yourself

- Think of something that is draining your energy right now. (Choose from the list above.)

- Let your imagination flow and notice what you feel, think, imagine doing, and/or picture.

- How do you suppose those things are connected?

Does this help you see what might be triggering your distress?

We'll talk more about how others have done this in Chapter 6.

CHAPTER FOUR

YOUR PAST MATTERS

Let It Go

> – Robert Lopez, Kristen Anderson-Lopez,
> Emanuel Kiriakou

It would be so nice to be able to never go back and let the past stay in the past. It just doesn't work that way.

Stories teach us that healing takes work. In the extremely popular and successful Disney film, "Frozen," the heroine, Elsa, lives a painful journey and travels through deep despair before she declares her freedom.

Several years ago Brian Klemmer, an experienced change facilitator, wrote a book titled, *If How-Tos Were Enough We Would All Be Skinny, Rich and Happy.* If you have ever experienced being unsuccessful at following someone's instructions to "Just let it go!" often spoken in annoyance, you know that it takes more than willpower to let go of some kinds of distress.

That is true even if you really, really, really want to let it go. Somehow things seem to stick to you: hurt feelings because of real or imagined mistreatment, the thought of something bad happening to someone you love or a song you just can't seem to get out of your head. You even tell yourself "Forgive and forget, just let it go, just move on," but it's hard to do.

Holding On is Easier than Letting Go

The truth is that you have not been taught to use "letting go tools." In fact, you come into the world with "holding on tools." Your brain has evolved for survival! It notices every source of danger and stores it (or freezes it) so that you can quickly recognize danger without having to stop and think about it. It is automatic.

Automatic was wonderful when our human race evolved in the jungle and a fraction of a second could literally keep our ancestors from being eaten. The ones with the best programming survived and eventually produced you and me who live in a world with far different challenges. Part of the stress and anxiety you experience is your automatic brain responding to what it thinks is an emergency when your rational mind knows it is just a minor annoyance.

Many books describe this phenomenon. My favorite explanation is in the first chapter of Daniel Goleman's classic book, *Emotional Intelligence*. He calls it "brain hijacking." I sometimes think of it as an autopilot.

Setting your autopilot is a way to make certain you hold on to protective decisions you have made over the course of your life. Holding on is always easier than letting go. We all hold on by leaving bits of our energy with memories of painful experiences to keep them from intruding into our everyday lives. Those were the experiences we did not have the resources to manage at the time they happened.

You Try to Protect Yourself by Holding On

It takes some of your energy to hold on or freeze your negative experiences, and that energy gets stuck in place and isn't available for you to use to handle whatever is in front of you right now. So, paradoxically, something you did to protect yourself in the past causes a problem in your present life.

Sometimes we don't have those resources simply because we are powerless children in a world of grownups. Sometimes it's because the adults who should have been able to protect us are not immediately available for a variety of benign or traumatic reasons.

One toddler wandered a few feet away from his watching mother and encountered a stress that was toxic for him that other children usually did not find stressful at all. He simply saw a clown who was there to entertain children. The toddler was terrified and inconsolable and set his autopilot to protect him from these dangerous creatures. That protection lasted for years and the autopilot was very difficult to reset.

Sometimes we are overwhelmed by trauma which no ordinary human can manage. This often happens to military personnel who serve in war zones and to the first responders who protect us as police, firefighters and medical professionals. When we encounter too many losses in a short period of time and can't process them, we tend to freeze energy around them to protect ourselves from feeling the pain of our experiences.

Sometimes we hold on to something because it is incomplete and we want a satisfactory ending. This can be especially problematic when the person or event with whom we want to complete something is long gone from our lives, either because they have died or have changed so much that the original just no longer exists. It's like wanting to complete something with a 30-year-old parent who is now 80 years old and does not even remember the incident that you have held on to for 50 years.

The more things you are holding on to, the more likely it is that some of them will be reactivated by the ordinary stress of just living. That's when we sometimes experience anxiety or depression that seems to have no particular cause.

Letting Go is Challenging

Resetting your autopilot and releasing the frozen energy can be time consuming and challenging. Spiritually based systems such as prayer and meditation have been developed over hundreds, even thousands of years to help cope with this problem. Many types of psychotherapy teach clients to change their reactions to current stress. Some kinds of psychotherapy try to reprogram brain connections. New energy therapies seem to do that also. One of these, "Tapping" in its various forms, is currently very popular.

Some of these technologies relieve your distressing reactions without any attempt to learn what caused your distress. Logosynthesis does ask the question, "What originally caused those reactions?" That is because the goal is to free the frozen energy that is used to hold on to the protection from the original situation and return it to where it belongs now.

At the same time this is done, the original problem that was so overwhelming when there were not enough resources to manage it becomes ordinary and even insignificant in relationship to currently available resources.

You can use the Logosynthesis sentences as another way of resetting your automatic pilot. The "you" that does the job is not the same you as the "you" who is reading this book and trying to manage your stress and anxiety. It is your essential inner "true Self." Some people think of it as the "you" that is connected to all that is. I won't attempt to define this any further. Just know that in the sentences that follow "I" means that part of you.

These sentences have been developed and revised since Dr. Willem Lammers discovered the basic principles of Logosynthesis in 2005.

Dr. Lammers is a therapist and coach who is highly trained in many different modalities. Once, while consulting on a difficult case, he observed that the client was referring to a part of herself as if it actually existed in the space next to her. When he invited the client to rejoin with this form in space, everything changed very suddenly.

You can read details of this story in his book, *Self Coaching with Logosynthesis: How the Power of Words Can Change Your Life*, for far more information than I am including here. If this process appeals to you, I highly recommend that you get it and study it in detail. For now, use this quick guide to get started.

The Logosynthesis Sentences Help You Let Go

These are the specific English words that are currently used by Logosynthesis practitioners. Other versions in several different languages can be found on the internet at www.Logosynthesis.net.

1. I retrieve all my energy bound up in (this—whatever your target is) and take it back to the right place in my Self.

2. I remove all the non-me energy related to (this—whatever your target is) from all of my cells, from my body and from my personal space and send it to where it truly belongs.

3. I retrieve all my energy bound up in all my reactions to (this—whatever your target is) and take it back to the right place in my Self.

You can see that without a target, the sentences are not useful. You will find much more detail about targets further on in this book. This is a simple description of how the sentences are used.

If you are working with a helper (professional or study-partner) your partner will read you the sentences in short chunks and you will repeat each chunk aloud. If you are working alone you may read the sentences or say them from memory.

You speak these words aloud and after each sentence you sit, pause for at least 15 seconds, breathe quietly, and notice what is happening in your body-mind system. You may feel muscles that want to tense or move, see pictures of events and people from your past, hear sounds or conversation and feel many different emotions and/or physical sensations. Or you may feel nothing at all.

All of these responses are completely normal. Simply notice what they are and let them pass naturally. When you feel complete with one sentence, move on to the next one. Repeat the process of saying the sentence, pausing, breathing and noticing what occurs.

When you have completed all three sentences notice how your feelings and perceptions of your target have changed. Doing this process with your first target may help you discover that another target would work more effectively to help you recover your energy from whatever is causing you distress. If so, repeat the process using the new target.

When all of your energy is back where it belongs and you are no longer troubled by energy coming from outside yourself, say sentence 4.

4. I tune all of my systems to this new awareness.

That is the basic process of using Logosynthesis, either alone or with a helper.

It is much easier to use it with a helper who can read you the sentences in small chunks which you repeat aloud. That allows you to stay focused on your experience instead of needing to switch your focus back and forth from reading.

It sounds amazingly simple, doesn't it? However, some additional information will help you understand how to find the targets you need to use it successfully.

CHAPTER FIVE

WORDS ARE POWERFUL

Every story I create, creates me.

– Octavia

You set up your own autopilot by telling yourself stories about what you encounter in the world. Making up stories is completely natural part of being human. Believing those stories is what causes problems. Getting committed to the stories is even more difficult to deal with. Once you have made up a story that seems to make sense, it does not occur to you that another story might describe your situation more accurately.

Listening to the stories you tell yourself is one of the ways you can discover where your energy is stuck.

You start creating stories almost as soon as you learn to talk. One problem with that is the resources you have to explain the world to yourself when you are a preschooler are very limited. Your brain is developing and sees everything very concretely. Since your sense of your own power is very over-rated, you often take personal credit or blame for causing situations that, in reality, are completely beyond your control.

This Story Led to Toxic Stress

Emily created a story as a child that influenced her entire life. Just imagine this scene and you will understand how easy it is to do.

Four-year-old Emily is angry at her mother and yells, "You're a bad mommy!" Mother, pregnant, frustrated and exhausted herself, snaps back, "Be quiet, you are giving me a headache!" (I know that is not good parenting, but unfortunately it is all too common.)

Later when mother has severe morning sickness, Emily is scared because she knows that something is very wrong but does not understand what it is. Her immature mind figures out that if she can give mother a headache, she must be responsible for this problem too. After all, she still thinks angry thoughts when things don't go her way.

Emily tells herself this story: "I'm a bad girl because I made mommy sick." She then decides that from now on, she should be good and not make any demands or complaints and essentially freezes the exuberant, demanding, alive part of herself.

As a responsible and successful grownup woman, Emily has long since forgotten that she once created this story, but the story she now tells herself is about how much she is supposed to be doing. She exhausts herself by trying to take care of everything and everyone around her. She feels stressed and anxious about managing all the demands of her busy life.

How Words Help Target and Release the Toxic Stress

This is where the Logosynthesis sentences can help relieve her stress, but first she needs a target.

In a workshop exercise to find targets to use for practice, she describes feeling stressed because she has to take a business trip and set up all the meals and activities for her husband and school-age children before she leaves. When looking for a target for the sentences her group decides it is "this belief that I am responsible for doing everything."

This is how the sentences she used were constructed to help her relieve her stress.

1. I retrieve all my energy bound up in (this belief that I am responsible for doing everything) and take it back to the right place in my Self.

2. I remove all the non-me energy related to (this belief that I am responsible for doing everything) from all of my cells, from my body and from my personal space and send it to where it truly belongs.

3. I retrieve all my energy bound up in all my reactions to (this belief that I am responsible for doing everything) and take it back to the right place in my Self.

Since this was a workshop situation, a partner was readily available. Emily sat quietly with her eyes closed and repeated the words as phrases that were given to her in this form.

1. *Helper:* I retrieve all my energy

   Emily: I retrieve all my energy

   Helper: bound up in this belief

   Emily: bound up in this belief

Helper: that I am responsible for doing everything

Emily: that I am responsible for doing everything

Helper: and take it back to the right place in my Self.

Emily: and take it back to the right place in my Self.

Emily sits quietly for about 30 seconds and a variety of expressions cross her face. She opens her eyes and nods at her helper. Her helper proceeds with sentence 2.

2. *Helper:* I remove all the non-me energy

   Emily: I remove all the non-me energy

   Helper: related to this belief

   Emily: related to this belief

Helper: that I am responsible for doing everything

Emily: that I am responsible for doing everything

Helper: from all of my cells,

Emily: from all of my cells,

Helper: from my body and from my personal space

Emily: from my body and from my personal space

Helper: and send it to where it truly belongs.

Emily: and send it to where it truly belongs.

Again Emily sits with her eyes closed and shifts her position several times. After about 45 seconds she looks at her helper and says "Okay." Her helper proceeds with sentence 3.

3. *Helper:* I retrieve all my energy bound up in all my reactions to this belief

    Emily: I retrieve all my energy bound up in all my reactions to this belief

    Helper: that I am responsible for doing everything

    Emily: that I am responsible for doing everything

    Helper: and take it back to the right place in my Self.

    Emily: and take it back to the right place in my Self.

Emily sits with her eyes closed for about a minute and finally opens them and looks at her helper. Her helper asks her what she experienced. Emily says that she feels much more relaxed but kept having memories of trying to take care of her mother when she was small.

This is a workshop, so Emily does not go further at that moment. She notes that for further work she can focus on these experiences in her early life. Her helper then offered her sentence 4 as a way of acknowledging her relaxation even though there was still more work to do in this area.

Helper: I tune all of my systems to this new awareness.

Emily: I tune all of my systems to this new awareness.

In the workshop, it is time for someone else to practice. You can, of course, read the sentences aloud yourself and pause between sentences and notice what you experience as your Self processes the words. Many people need to remind themselves to allow time for this processing.

Your Past Influences Today's Stories

When Emily was 4, she didn't know what to do about her mother's illness and unavailability so she froze that bit of her angry and confused energy and created a story. The story she created was about being responsible for taking care of her mother because she had made mother sick.

As Emily matured, she translated her story, with the help of other information from her surroundings into the story that she had to take care of everyone else in order to be accepted. And it seemed to work, until it filled up all her available time and led to overwhelming anxiety that she could not keep up with the load she had imposed upon herself.

What happened to you in the past influences the stories you continue to tell yourself throughout your life. Since you often created the stories in response to stressful or uncomfortable situations they may no longer be useful to you. In any case, they serve to separate you from your true Self.

I often remind my clients that everyone creates stories. That is how we are built as humans. The problem comes when we believe that the stories are true and act accordingly. Before I learned Logosynthesis, I suggested to my clients that when you are caught up in a story that explains your world, you can experiment with creating more stories that explain the situation in different ways. Sometimes creating silly or extreme stories helps you recognize how arbitrary the stories actually are.

That process is still useful but does not reset your automatic pilot. The Logosynthesis process can help you release those stories that cause you distress and can help you release the energy stuck in the story and all it represents. The process also allows you to become more aware of who you really are at your Essence—your true Self.

Targeting the Original Story

The part of Emily's use of Logosynthesis you saw took her back to the original story. We store our stories as pictures or patterns that contain much more information than the words we use to describe the story.

Imagine looking at a snapshot. If you try to describe it in words you may focus on the people in it, the activity they are engaged in, the environment or even the memories it evokes. That is why her next step involves describing the memory of trying to take care of her mother when she was only about 4 years old.

Once Emily has remembered as many details of the snapshot as she can (including sounds, smells, colors, relative positions of objects, etc.) she identifies where she perceives it in her personal space.

That may seem a bit strange, so take a moment and try this experiment. It may help to close your eyes after you read the instructions. Imagine your own mother in the space you are in right now.

- Where is she?

- Is she in front of you?

- Is she behind you?

- Is she in the doorway?

- How far away is she?

- How do you know?

- What is she doing?

- Is she looking at you?

- Do you see her face? Her profile?

- Do you notice anything else?

Now do you see how it exists in your personal space?

Emily can use the snapshot memory as the target the next time she uses the three sentences to release the energy she froze when she was only 4 years old.

Finding targets is the biggest challenge for most people who want to use Logosynthesis to relieve stress and anxiety. That's what we will focus on next.

CHAPTER SIX

FIND YOUR TARGET

Dear Stress, Let's Break Up.

– Pinterest

You can't really break up with stress. After all it is an important part of life. You grow by responding to stress. When you need to stretch to respond to something you increase your capacity in that area. However, what you can do is reclaim the energy you are using to protect yourself from your reactions to toxic stress in your recent and distant past and in your imagined future.

Finding the target really means searching your body, your memory and the physical space that surrounds you to discover the bits of energy you froze around this stress. You froze your energy in order to protect yourself from the pain and overwhelm you experienced then. You may also be losing energy by imagining that similar painful events will occur in the future.

You may be very aware that your energy is stuck in toxic stress you are currently trying to manage in your life. On the other hand you may know your energy is stuck because you feel vague, nagging, hard to figure out or explain, anxiety or depression or a whole variety of other symptoms. In any case, in order to use the Logosynthesis sentences to reclaim that energy you need to describe what triggers your distress.

When the trigger is deactivated, the memory of the stressful event will remain but your reaction to the memory changes. It may seem as if the stress magically disappears but what really disappears is the block you once created that kept your energy from flowing freely.

Searching for Your Target

Your challenge now is to explore places in your life where your energy is stuck in order to focus the power of your true Self to allow the powerful words of the Logosynthesis sentences to dissolve the frozen energy.

In Chapter 3 you learned about some common clues to frozen energy. If you know you are experiencing some out-of-proportion reactions in your life right now, start there. Answering these two questions will help you find a target to use.

First answer this question, "How are you uncomfortable right now?" It could be about a relationship, your work, your health or your aspirations. Looking at what you can't stop thinking about or what you avoid because it scares you or makes you very uncomfortable may help you answer that question.

Your current discomfort may be an emotion such as anxiety which is a form of fear, or anger or sadness. Emotions are temporary and change as circumstances change so they do not make good targets. They do often suggest where to look further to locate your target.

Your next question is, "What did you experience (think about, feel, notice) just before you experienced your current discomfort?" Often this is a real or imagined event. A snapshot of the most uncomfortable or stressful part of this remembered or imagined event makes an excellent target.

Don't worry if you have trouble answering these questions now. As you review the following examples, you'll see how others responded to the questions. You can use their chosen targets as models for your own.

Target: A Stressful Event

This story is about me responding to a stressful event.

Recently I found myself losing my composure during a telephone conversation with the driver of a car that had rear-ended my stopped car earlier in the day. I had made the mistake of not calling the police at the time because the damage was minor.

She had promised to call with the missing insurance information later in the day. She did not call. Instead, she avoided my calls and when she finally did respond she accused me of harassing her. When I asked for her insurance information so I could report the damage she raised her voice and implied that I was trying to get her into trouble.

The answer to the first question seems obvious. I was nearly in tears and desperately wanted to verbally attack her, but I knew that doing so would only make the situation worse.

Fortunately, my husband was there and I asked him to take over the call. He had no reaction at all to her belligerence and calmed her down enough to get the information we needed. The answer to the second question also seems obvious. The unpleasant telephone call triggered my distress.

Using "this telephone call" as the target I said the sentences aloud and got a very clear image of an incident that happened when I was 16 years old. The image was me, staring fixedly at a black crack between two white tiles on the floor, feeling guilty and frozen, while my father yelled at me for making a mistake.

The really important target was the snapshot of "this image of the crack on the floor" because it represented so much frozen energy from the past. Once I said the sentences with that new target I relaxed completely.

Yes, I did file a police report and her insurance did pay to have the damage repaired. And I had no particular emotional response to writing this account of the incident.

Target: Replaying a Recent Memory

Here's another example, a story, of someone replaying a memory of a recent event.

Yvonne invited her daughter and son-in-law to an expensive restaurant to celebrate his birthday. Instead of ordering entrées and desserts as she had expected, they each ordered several expensive appetizers, along with their entrées and desserts. A lot of the extra food was left uneaten, on the table.

She felt angry and taken advantage of, but couldn't figure out what to do about the situation. She replayed it in her mind over and over again, and complained to friends, "I just can't get it out of my head."

Yvonne's answer to question one was "this scene that is stuck in my head." Her answer to what happened just before she replayed the scene was that she felt angry because she had been taken advantage of. Feelings are normally temporary and don't make good targets. Her target was "this belief about how they should have behaved at the restaurant."

After she completed the sentences with this target she said calmly, "I won't be inviting them to any more meals in expensive restaurants."

Target: A Common Problem: Public Speaking

Here is an example of a common problem.

Tim had just taken a new position as a manager.

He was terrified about being required to give a presentation to four people at work. As he struggled to prepare it, he kept thinking about the time he forgot his lines in the school play and how embarrassed he was that day.

Tim knew the answer to the second question and his target was "this image of forgetting the lines in the play." After dissolving this image he was surprised that he actually enjoyed preparing and making his presentation.

Target: A Mysterious Reaction

This example was a mystery that needed to be unraveled.

Carolyn was very distressed at the idea of retiring from her successful career and couldn't figure out why. She had invested well and had ample resources to stop working without it having any impact on her lifestyle at all. She wanted to retire and spend more time with her already retired husband. Still, every time she thought about retirement, she was terrified of not having enough money.

She told me, "Taking money to the bank means that it disappears." We used the statement, "this belief that taking money to the bank means that it disappears" as the target.

When she said the sentences she realized that her belief was connected to a time when her parents promised to put money she earned into the bank for her to use for college. They spent the money for their own needs and never returned it to her.

Her old belief was a reality in her past experience. Money did disappear when she put it in the bank then, but that belief had nothing to do with her current reality. She dissolved the belief and is thoroughly enjoying her retirement.

Target: A Fantasy About the Future

A common problem is that your protective brain imagines that a problem or situation that happened in the past will be repeated and does its best to keep you out of trouble.

Marie was told repeatedly by the Nuns at school that it was important to dress modestly. She never broke the rules. As an adult, she is very uncomfortable wearing the attractive, stylish clothing her friends enjoy. Her target was "this fantasy that the Nuns will punish me." After she finished saying the sentences she announced that she was going shopping.

Target: An Attempt to Change the Past

You can also create toxic stress by repeatedly trying to solve an impossible problem like getting a dead parent to change something she did when she was alive.

Ron often replayed the scene of his mother giving away his comic books, told others the story and insisted that he could never forgive her, even though she had died 10 years earlier. We suggested that he could retrieve his energy from "this belief that mother should have been different."

After he used that target in the sentences he said, "She was only 27 and had three kids in a one-bedroom apartment."

More Sample Targets

Here is a list of 50 other targets used by real people in some of our workshops.

1. This image of her standing there screaming at me (the employee having a major freak out).

2. The voice of (a person in memory) scolding me.

3. This belief that I should be able to handle negativity.

4. This weight on my shoulders (the migraine pain that takes me out of my life).

5. This pressure, tension and tightness in my chest.

6. All of the times when I haven't been heard.

7. The time I wasn't listened to.

8. This belief that I'm supposed to be in charge of this process.

9. All of the fantasies that get in the way of my writing.

10. This fantasy that I won't succeed. (Belief that I'm not enough.)

11. This turning in my gut (experiencing something as unnerving and gross).

12. This traumatic image in my mind (image of doing CPR on the dying person).

13. This fantasy that business will use up all of my time and I won't enjoy it.

14. The fantasy that I can get what I missed from my father (trying to retrieve father's wisdom from his papers).

15. This experience of being locked out of my heart.

16. This scene of finding (name) (previously finding someone who had suicided by gunshot).

17. The fantasy of all the terrible things that will happen if I lose my home.

18. This fantasy of not being able to give something of value.

19. This sore, warm acid lump in my gut.

20. The expectation of how my daughter should behave (daughter is a drug addict).

21. This residual heartache.

22. This image of (name) driving away with the wire attached to my heart.

23. His voice saying I'm selfish.

24. Picture of (name) walking away from the table.

25. This language that's stuck in the back of my head.

26. All the distractions that keep me from my project.

27. My mother's voice telling me I should be doing something different.

28. All the obstacles to achieving this task.

29. These bodies pushing in on me and squashing me (discomfort with airplane travel).

30. This decision to take care of everything.

31. Mother telling me I was no good right after I had been raped.

32. The sense that I'm toxic.

33. This image of my daughter (name) choosing to live her life their way.

34. This image of being alone with my father.

35. This need for my mother's sympathy.

36. This image of me in the dressing room mirror.

37. This danger that I remember (probably being molested as a child).

38. This food that's calling to me.

39. Whatever is between me and my memory (forgets important things).

40. The belief that I don't deserve to accomplish what I want to.

41. The burden of this responsibility.

42. My stepfather calling me fat at age 12.

43. All of this stuff (this overwhelming clutter of objects).

44. This sticky energy in front of me.

45. This image of the compass.

46. This image of Jack's ball (Adam's apple).

47. This belief that something bad will happen if I mess with this.

48. The image of sitting inside my father.

49. Everything involved with protecting myself from my father.

50. The image of my mother combing my hair.

Notice that many targets start with the word 'this' instead of the word 'my.' Since you want to release the image or belief you are more likely to let it go if you don't claim ownership of it with your words.

Remember, if the target you choose to work with isn't exactly right, the next target often becomes obvious as soon as you use the first one in the sentences. If you find yourself feeling overwhelmed if you think about any particular target, do not address it right away. Choose something that is easier.

There are no mistakes and no wrong answers. You have plenty of time to experiment and often learn lots about yourself in the process.

CHAPTER SEVEN

WHY DOES THIS WORK?

Any sufficiently advanced technology is indistinguishable from magic.

— Arthur C. Clarke

The late science writer and futurist, Clarke's full quote is:

When a distinguished but elderly scientist states that something is possible, he is almost certainly right. When he states that something is impossible, he is very probably wrong. The only way of discovering the limits of the possible is to venture a little way past them into the impossible. Any sufficiently advanced technology is indistinguishable from magic.

You don't really need to understand much about how Logosynthesis works to use it to relieve the toxic stress, anxiety, depression, procrastination and over-reactiveness or other distress you experience. You do need to take the perspective that those problems are all involved with the location and flow of your own energy.

Are you skeptical? From many other perspectives, this process makes no sense at all. Nor do several kinds of energy work that have been in use for centuries. From those same perspectives, prayer should not work either—but I have encountered some controlled research that shows that it does impact healing.

I have heard various explanations about why this process works and they all depend on believing things I don't fully understand. I also drive a car, take prescription medication, use my cellphone, the micro-wave oven and the Internet and I don't fully understand those processes either. I still accept that I can benefit from using them.

After my first encounters with Logosynthesis showed me the incredible power of the right words said with the intention to help me and others make significant changes in our lives, I became a believer. I hope you will at least suspend your skepticism long enough to experiment and see for yourself what actually happens.

The Words Are Important

The specific wording of the sentences and the order in which the sentences are used has been refined over the 10 years since Willem Lammers' discovery of this process. Groups of professionals have used and discussed the impact of how to use the words and there are continuous new developments—in several different languages. The website Logosynthesis.net has up-to-date infor-mation.

When you look at life challenges from an energy viewpoint, this does fit together and seems to work well both as a professional tool and in self-coaching situ-ations.

The Sentence Order Is Deliberate

Sentence one is used to strengthen you by taking back energy that has been unavailable to you for a variety of reasons. Those reasons have usually focused on avoiding reminders of past distress and possible future difficulties instead of living in the present moment. Once you have taken back your own energy you are ready for the next step.

Sentence two lets your Self release the energy you have taken in from other people or objects in your environment. When you are vulnerable, you often accept energy from others. A good example of holding someone else's energy is when you find yourself saying something one of your parents said to you that you swore never to repeat. After you have reclaimed your own energy by using sentence one you can then use sentence two to remove that energy you no longer need or want to hold onto.

Most of what you describe as problems in your life now are the reactions you experience when you try to avoid thinking about, remembering or re-experiencing the discomfort you tried to protect yourself from in the first place. In other words, the solutions that seemed to make sense in the past become the problems of today.

Once you have used the first two sentences to straighten out your energy around your original protective actions, the third sentence is designed to move the energy from your reactions to that original protection back to where you need it—the right place in your Self.

It's About the Energy, Not the Story

Since you are working with your energy and not your story when using Logosynthesis, this is a lot easier than it sounds here. You create your story as a way to make sense of the world you experience—everybody does. Three people exposed to the same event usually create different stories.

I once had a vivid reminder of this in my own life. I grew up in a family that was mostly loving and supportive but imperfect as all families are. From my current perspective, I can tell myself the story that my father was the somewhat indulged youngest of seven children. Sometimes, when he did not get his own way he yelled almost as if he was a four-year-old having a temper tantrum.

After my father died, my sister, my brother and I were reminiscing about growing up with his occasionally yelling at us. When he yelled, the story I told myself from the time I was a small child until I was in my 40s was that something was wrong with me that I needed to correct. The story my sister told herself was that her father was being silly and she could ignore him until he calmed down again. The story my brother told himself was that his father was angry and should be avoided. It was the same father.

Since I couldn't cope with his yelling, I apparently froze a lot of energy about my experiences of it in order to protect myself. I was amazed when I learned that my siblings had so little reaction to the same events.

Since your stories are rather arbitrary, in this kind of work they are important only to point you to where your energy is frozen so you can create an appropriate target to work with. Then you no longer need the stories and you certainly do not need to go deeply into the most painful parts of the stimulus for those stories.

Note: If your stories are about events that newspapers would now call child abuse, or other trauma, it would be better to do this work with a trained professional. A guide to resources is at the end of the book. Logosynthesis in the hands of a trained professional has more complexity than I am describing here. As a professional myself, I experience it as a banquet. I am giving you more of a fast food version to help you manage ordinary toxic stress and anxiety and other everyday problems.

One of the most common mistakes almost everyone seems to make when learning to use this process is to focus too much on those stories we use to justify our reactions to our frozen energy. We frequently need to remind our workshop participants and clients that "It's not about the story."

Experience Using Logosynthesis

It's time to try it for yourself.

You can do this either alone or with a partner. All you need is about 20 minutes of uninterrupted time and a location where you can speak aloud without disturbing others. Read through to the end of this chapter before you start.

Here is a very brief summary of the highlights of this process.

A (Very) Brief Guide to Using Logosynthesis

Logosynthesis is a model for guided change that uses three important sentences, spoken aloud:

The "I" in each sentence refers to your Essence—the part of you that is an expression of all that is—your Higher Self—your true Self. Some might call it 'basic goodness' and others call it your soul.

A brief statement of "your target" goes in the brackets in each sentence. Your target is a memory, fantasy or belief that is related to your frozen energy and is causing you distress. It could be whatever you can't get out of your mind or "makes you crazy" or distracts you or keeps you from connecting to your Essence.

Say each sentence out loud; pause between the sentences and notice what thoughts, feelings, images, etc., come to you. Don't try to understand the meaning of the sentences, just let the words work.

1. I retrieve all my energy bound up in (this— your target) and return it to the right place in my Self.

2. I remove all the not-me energy related to (this—your target) from all of my cells, from my body, and from my personal space, and send it to wherever it truly belongs.

3. I retrieve all my energy bound up in all my reactions to (this—your target) and return it to the right place in my Self.

Once you feel that your energy has shifted, say this:

4. I tune all of my systems to this new awareness.

Now It's Your Turn

Here is a much more detailed guide to get you started.

Remember, some people experience an intense reaction to these words and others experience almost nothing. Sometimes I experience no reaction at the time I do the work but a day or a week later I notice that the problem I was addressing has disappeared. There is NO INCORRECT RESPONSE!

First, prepare for your experiment.

- Create a copy of the sentences that you can use as a guide. If you use this process frequently you will eventually memorize the sentences but you do NOT need to do this before you start.

- Have some water available to drink. Drinking water seems to facilitate doing energy work.

- Decide on a target to use for this practice session. Start small—if you were rating your distress on a scale of 1-10 with 1 being barely noticeable and 10 being overwhelming, choose a target you would rate no higher than 7.

- Extra. If you like to keep track of your own growth process, do keep a record of the targets you work with in a permanent Logosynthesis Journal. Otherwise any scraps of paper will work.

- Write out your target. Writing will help you to both clarify it for yourself and remember exactly what it is as you practice.

- Extra. Sometimes it helps to write the entire Logosynthesis sentence with the target as part of it. Sometimes that is way too much trouble. You decide what will work for you.

- Write the number that rates your level of distress with this target.

Follow this procedure to do your first experiment.

- Say the first sentence. If you are working alone say sentence one that contains your target aloud. If you are working with a partner, use the method of speak and respond described in Chapter 5.

- Sit calmly and notice how you respond to this experience. It is counter-productive to try to remember the words you have just spoken aloud. You probably won't be able to anyway. TAKE YOUR TIME and let your thoughts and feelings that come as words, visual images, smells, sounds or speech and/or the physical sensations you experience just go by. Just notice them. Don't rush this process.

- Make sure you wait at least 15 seconds before moving on. You may experience nothing or anything at all. There is no right or wrong response—anything is fine.

- Repeat the process using sentences two and three.

- When you feel complete with sentence three, notice and write down the number that describes your level of distress right now. Notice whether it has changed from the first number you recorded.

- If your target was some sort of snapshot image, check the image and see how it may have changed.

- If your level of distress is at least 2 points lower than when you started, say the fourth sentence aloud.

- Drink several sips of water.

- If you are keeping a Logosynthesis Journal, write a sentence about your experience.

Use this process as often as you like for any different targets you discover.

In the next and last chapter you'll find tips and tricks that others have found useful in their practice of Logosynthesis.

CHAPTER EIGHT

YES, YOU CAN!

In theory there is no difference between theory and practice. In practice there is.

– Yogi Berra and others

Y ou can do this! You can learn to use this tool for your own growth. Like any tool, you will get no benefit from it if you leave it on the shelf to gather dust. You do need to practice, so go ahead and get started. Are you intrigued by the possibilities? Here are some tips and tricks to insure your success.

If a professional has suggested that you read this, it makes sense to follow his or her suggestions for guided self-growth. If you are curious about what you can do on your own, the answer is basically, experiment! There are no rules.

The best possible outcome is total spiritual awakening and transformation. Using the process can help lead you to a joy-filled life. The worst thing that will happen is nothing at all. Fortunately, this is a very low risk process. Even if nothing much happens, all you will lose is a few minutes of your time.

Probably your experience will be somewhere between these extremes. Here are suggestions to help make your experiments as productive as possible.

Practice Your Way

Get accustomed to using the tool before you need it for something really intense or important.

Just learning about Logosynthesis is not enough to enable you to let go of the toxic stress and anxiety in your life. If you want this process to work for you, you will need to practice using it to let go of small stresses in your daily life.

Toxic stress and anxiety often seem to reinforce each other. It is hard to tell which comes first. Practicing using the sentences in mild stress situations helps you become comfortable using the tool at more distressing times.

Shawn decided to practice the sentences whenever he felt annoyed in traffic. Not only did he calm himself, he discovered an impatient part of himself that got in the way of his goal of getting closer to his family.

When you feel stressed because you don't have time to meet your own high standards, you can use that as an opportunity to practice saying the sentences and reclaiming your energy from the situation.

Lois was expecting guests for dinner but unexpectedly needed to work late. There was simply no time to prepare the dessert she had planned. She solved the problem by purchasing some ice cream on the way home. Instead of feeling relief she created her own stress by internally berating herself for not taking the time to prepare the dessert the day before. This is a good example of a perfect, low risk opportunity to practice.

She decided that a good target would be "this fantasy that I should be able to predict the future." She whispered the sentences while she was waiting in line at the supermarket and felt more relaxed.

In a much more stressful situation the next week, when the coach of her son's team called to tell her there was an important make-up game in another town on the same day that she had promised to celebrate her mother's birthday, she was more prepared to help herself step away from her stress.

She recognized that she was starting to feel anxious about being exposed to another guilt trip if she tried to reschedule the time with her mother.

YES, YOU CAN! 115

She used the sentences on the (imagined) image of her mother expressing bitter disappointment at the change of plans. She was calm later when she did talk to her mother who decided to join them for the game.

Use Your Technical Aids

Use the tools you already have to help you.

The sooner you can use the sentences without stopping to read them, the better. You can enter them into your phone so you can read them frequently and memorize them. Be sure to download your free gift listed at the end of this chapter. It contains phone-ready images you can easily photograph.

You can also read the sentences aloud into a recording app in chunks, just like a partner would, so you can just repeat the chunks using your own target.

Keep your photo or recording instantly available to remind you of the process instead of having to search for this book or your notes when you need them.

Let Your Self Take Charge

You can't control what happens! Get used to it and relax.

There is a part of you, your ego, which is doing its best to run your life based on your past experiences and the stories you tell yourself. That part of you may say things like "I don't know where the right place within myself is located." It may also tell you to be sure to remember and repeat the words to yourself—over and over again. Your ego is interested in CONTROL! Its theme may be "I can do it myself!"

That is not what this process is about. This process is about helping your ego let go and engaging the guidance of your Self, the deepest part of your being, the very Essence of you, to care for you and lead you to the life you wish for. Your Self has your best interests at heart but may organize things in an order or direction you don't expect. Just notice your responses to what happens.

When you say the sentences, don't expect anything in particular to happen. Just be observant and notice what does happen. You may sometimes experience intense emotions, physical sensations or movements, or deep peace, or absolutely nothing. These responses are simply signals that energy is moving. They usually pass quickly. There is no right way to do this and there are no wrong answers or experiences.

Take Your Time

Your energy moves while the words impact your systems. This may take anywhere from 15 seconds to several minutes or even longer. Your ego may attempt to take control again by deciding that nothing important is happening and urge you do go on to the next sentence. When you cut the process short, you are less likely to gain the benefits of your practice.

If you sit quietly with your eyes closed and just notice thoughts, feelings, memories, sounds, smells, images, sensations, etc., you give your energy time to move back to the place where it belongs. You will learn to notice when the energy flow seems to settle and nothing more happens. Then it is time for the next sentence.

Use Images When You Can

Images are stronger targets than just words.

An image, like a snapshot, has lots of information contained in it. It often represents a time when you froze some of your energy in response to stress. It has the things you pay attention to and those that you don't but are still aware of. You can get a sense of this by looking around. What do you notice? What else is there?

The room I am in has several chairs, some stuffed animals and a few tables. I am more aware of what is happening on the computer screen than any of those things.

When you take your energy back from an image you carry, the image often changes and that shift may help you better understand yourself. An image does not need to be visual. It can be a memory of sounds or voices which also may represent a time and place where you froze a piece of your experience.

Words work too. If you have both words and images available to work with, choose the image.

Take Small Bites

Use small slices of an experience rather than the entire remembered experience as a target.

You may be more successful in releasing stress and anxiety from one piece of an event at a time. You could work with a small part of the entire scene like the thumping sound you heard or the look on someone's face. Dr. Lammers calls this slicing the salami.

When you work with one slice at a time, particularly when you are working with a distressing memory, your responses may be smaller and feel more manageable.

This quote sums it up for me. "Do it badly; do it slowly; do it fearfully; do it any way you have to, but do it." Steve Chandler, *Reinventing Yourself: How to Become the Person You've Always Wanted to Be.*

If you feel overwhelmed at any time, slow down. You can get professional help if you need it. There is a list of certified professionals in many different areas at Logosynthesis.net. Most of them will work with clients by phone or over the internet communication systems.

You can practice on your own or find a buddy to work with or both!

Use Your Imagination and Creativity

Although I have focused on using this process on reducing stress and anxiety, it is useful for many other challenges.

Irene was taking one of our classes when she decided to try it for procrastination. She had been putting off writing a series of papers she needed to complete a certification process and discovered that Logosynthesis can be an incredible aid to productivity. At one meeting, she surprised us by reporting that she had completed the reports in record time using the target "whatever is keeping me from finishing these papers."

Some people have successfully experimented with using the sentences to help with physical issues. Dr. Lammers has cured himself of hay fever using the process. I have been less successful but may have averted a few infections by retrieving my energy from "this inflammation."

I even find myself mumbling the sentences while I am brushing my teeth at night. That is when I seem to review my day and sometimes discover myself dwelling on left-over resentments I don't need or want. I am quite sure that taking my energy back from those resentments allows me sleep more soundly.

You can also use it as a tool for personal growth or even as a spiritual development process. If you choose the latter, scheduling regular practice is extremely helpful.

One problem I have noticed both in myself and in my students is that we tend to forget that we can use the sentences to help with the most stressful situations. That's right, we simply forget that the tool exists.

I am fortunate that my husband Jonathan and I learned to use this tool together. So now when I say I am frustrated with something or he notices that I am overreacting to some simple situation he suggests that I do the process or offers to help me with it. That is a real benefit of having a partner.

You may find it easier to make and keep appointments for practice sessions with a partner than with yourself. On the other hand, you may feel that this work is very private and not want to share it with anyone. You get to choose what will work best for you and to change it if you want to.

Choose Joy

It's not what happens that makes you feel stressed or anxious; it is how you respond to what you feel that makes the difference. Instead of holding on to suffering you can choose to use your own response to the toxic stress you encounter as a platform for your own growth.

Remember, you can't avoid all stress. Your goal is to let go of the effects of toxic stress and anxiety in your life and live as much as possible in the present moment.

The process is to use the Logosynthesis sentences to dissolve your triggers and make your energy available to you right now.

The joy, aliveness and freedom you will experience will be your reward.

Claim Your Free Gift Here

I have a special gift for you to make it easier for you to benefit from using Logosynthesis right away.

To receive your gift, just send an email to www.BooksByLaurie.com/guide and I'll let you know how to download your own copy of your *Quick Start Guide: Using Logosynthesis to Release Anxiety, Stress and Worry* by return email.

This report contains a special formatting of the three sentences that you can photograph with your phone and carry around with you.

May your life be filled with energy and joy!

Please Help Spread the Word

Dear Reader,

I hope you enjoyed *Letting It Go: Relieve Anxiety and Toxic Stress in Just a Few Minutes Using Only Words.* I have to tell you what a joy it is to share this information with you.

When I wrote the first few chapters the early feedback made me realize how many people this book could help to lead more joyful and relaxed lives. **I need your help** to let them know about it.

So, I need to ask a favor.

If you are so inclined, I'd love to have you write and post a review of *Letting It Go: Relieve Anxiety and Toxic Stress in Just a Few Minutes Using Only Words.* Loved it, found it useful, didn't care for it, intend to use it—help other potential readers learn about it by sharing what you think.

You, the reader, have the power to make or break a book with your reviews. If you have the time I would be honored if you will post your review on Amazon or Goodreads or wherever you share this information. To make it easier for you, here's a link to a listing of my books on Amazon. You can find all of my books here: www.BooksByLaurie.com.

Thank you so much for reading *Letting It Go: Relieve Anxiety and Toxic Stress in Just a Few Minutes Using Only Words* and for spending time with me.

With gratitude and appreciation,

Laurie

Laurie Weiss, Ph.D.

P.S. I would love to hear from you. My email address is;

LaurieWeiss@EmpowermentSystems.com

P.P.S. If you take an extra few minutes to let me know where and when you post your review, I will personally thank you for helping me reach new readers. Just drop me an email me at;

LaurieWeiss@EmpowermentSystems.com.

ACKNOWLEDGEMENTS

I am grateful for the help of many people for their support, encouragement and insight that has brought this book from an idea to a reality.

Many, many, many thanks to:

- Dr. Willem Lammers, who told me a book was needed to introduce Logosynthesis to people outside the professional community that was written in accessible and non-academic language and then asked if I would write it. As a newly certified Basic Logosynthesis Trainer I was honored that my expertise in translating complicated concepts into accessible language was being recognized. I appreciate his support and encouragement throughout every phase of this project.

- Dr. Jonathan B. Weiss, my husband since 1960 and business partner since 1972, for reading every word of the first draft of each chapter and helping with so many of the other technical and tedious tasks that are necessary to produce a book.

- Nancy Porter-Steele, who was one of the first people to introduce me to Logosynthesis and has encouraged me in every way and has generously edited this book manuscript as well.

- The members of the Little Logo Book Creation Facebook group who have offered support and feedback from at least eight different countries! I am so grateful to everyone who read and "liked" each chapter as I posted it and especially to those people who offered the useful feedback that helped me refine the language and concepts and reassure me that I was on target.

Special thanks goes to those members of the group who have taken the time to provide detailed and thoughtful feedback during this process: Pamela Burkhalter, Julie Jacinthe Arsenault, Foster Brashear, Trish North, Judy Heiser Warren, Karen Bartholow, Satinder Bhalla, Cathy Schenkels Caswell, and Cheryl Liang.

And special thanks go to my grandson, Ryan Claret, for his clear and thoughtful feedback from a teenager's perspective.

Finally, thank you for the invaluable advice and support of Judith Briles, Amy Collins and all my friends and colleagues at AuthorU.org throughout every phase of this project.

ABOUT THE AUTHOR

After over 40 years practicing psychotherapy and coaching, Dr. Laurie Weiss had no intention of starting a new phase of her career. Then a colleague helped her resolve a persistent, stressful problem using an amazing new technique. She was astounded that he did it in just a few minutes, while standing on the sidewalk outside of a restaurant, using only words.

Dr. Weiss was so intrigued with this recently discovered tool that she and her husband of over 50 years, Dr. Jonathan B Weiss, went to Nova Scotia, Canada to learn the technique. Using it, they were thrilled to help their clients make important life changes in a fraction of the time, and with a fraction of the pain ordinarily associated with psycho-therapy.

Four years and considerable studying later, they became the only Certified Logosynthesis® Practitioners and Basic Trainers in the United States.

As a teenager Dr. Weiss read science fiction stories about how ordinary people could do extraordinary things and was determined to find the right teachers to help her learn to do those things too. Studying with a variety of experts, she decided to make it easier for others learn to do what she had done.

She has long believed that ordinary people can learn to help themselves solve all kinds of problems if only they have the right tools. Throughout her professional life she has specialized in making those tools accessible to anyone who is interested. She brings to this book her expertise in writing in a way that makes complex professional information usable by ordinary people.

Laurie Weiss, Ph.D., is an expert in rapid stress and anxiety relief as well as in relationship communication. She loves helping very smart people stop making dumb relationship mistakes, and instead, repair those mistakes one transaction at a time.

Her professional background also includes certification as a Teaching and Supervising Transactional Analyst, International Transactional Analysis Association and Master Certified Coach, International Coach Federation.

She is a best-selling author of numerous books including *Recovery from Co-Dependency*, seven other books with spines and several additional ebooks and numerous articles. Her work has been translated into German, Chinese, Spanish, French, Portuguese and possibly Russian.

Her personal life has been intertwined with her professional life since she started working with her husband in 1970 when they moved their young family to Colorado. They have two children and five grand-children. Married in 1960, both Drs. Weiss have traveled extensively, teaching in 13 different countries.

They love mixing business and pleasure and have enjoyed visiting with professional colleagues and friends in North America and around the globe for many years. Lately they have discovered the delights of learning new things while cruising with friends and colleagues.

They live and work in Littleton, Colorado (USA).

HOW TO WORK WITH DR. LAURIE

My husband, Dr. Jonathan B. Weiss, and I have been married since 1960 and business partners since 1972 when we were teaching Transactional Analysis throughout the United States. We have been learning and teaching cutting-edge tools for healing and trans-formation for over 40 years.

Currently we are the only Certified Logosynthesis Practitioners in the United States. Either or both of us would be delighted to help you learn more about Logosynthesis and how to use it in your life and work.

You can find a list of Logosynthesis Practitioners who offer similar services throughout the world at www.Logosynthesis.net/docs/EN.pdf

Contact Us: We Usually Answer the Phone

You can contact us directly to discuss what is best for you and your group. We offer a variety of options including CLASSES, TALKS, BOOK GROUP VISITS, PROFESSIONAL CONFERENCE PRESENTATIONS, TRAINING, and INDIVIDUAL APPOINTMENTS. We work with our clients in person, by phone and by Skype.

Dr. Laurie Weiss:
LaurieWeiss@EmpowermentSystems.com

Dr. Jonathan Weiss:
Weiss@EmpowermentSystems.com

Empowerment Systems

506 West Davies Way

Littleton, CO 80120 USA

303.794.5379

Websites

Personal—www.LaurieWeiss.com

Logosynthesis—www.LogosynthesisColorado.com

Business—www.EmpowermentSystems.com

Purchase Books—www.BooksbyLaurie.com

Social Media

Facebook—www.Facebook.com/laurieweiss

LinkedIn—www.Linkedin.com/in/laurieweiss

Pinterest—www.Pinterest.com/laurieweiss/

Twitter—Twitter.com/@LaurieWeiss

Goodreads—www.Goodreads.com/Laurie_Weiss

Blogs

Personal Development—
www.IDontNeedTherapy.com/blog

Relationship—RelationshipHQ.com/blog/

Business Communication—
http://www.DareToSayIt.com/blog

LOGOSYNTHESIS RESOURCES

Organizations

Institute for Logosynthesis®:
www.Logosynthesis.net/

This is currently the central international site, with many resources, articles, training information, access to other languages, including the following:

- Audio File: An amazing new technique and system for personal development.

- The Logosynthesis® basic paper offers an introduction to the model for professionals.

- The Logosynthesis® Quick Reference paper gives you the most important information in a nutshell.

- Tips for Logosynthesis® in Coaching and Counselling.

- The Logosynthesis® Glossary provides definitions of the terms used.

- Presentation "Logosynthesis in a nutshell".

There is also a list of Certified Practitioners around the world:

www.Logosynthesis.net/docs/EN.pdf

International Logosynthesis® Association:

www.Logosynthesis.net/association-2/

This is the professional association in the process of formation.

Dr. Willem Lammers: info@Logosynthesis.net

Jonathan & Laurie Weiss:

www.LogosynthesisColorado.com

The Weisses are currently the only Certified Practitioners in the United States.

Books

Self Coaching with Logosynthesis®:

www.Logosynthesis.net/self-coaching-logosynthesis/

Logosynthesis®: Healing with Words: A Handbook for the Helping Professions:
www.Logosynthesis.net/logosynthesis-healing-with-words/

Restoring the Flow—a Primer in Logosynthesis :
www.Smashwords.com/books/view/284465/

Social Media

Facebook Group:
www.Facebook.com/groups/logosynthesis/

This is an open public group for people interested in knowing about Logosynthesis® events worldwide, and for newcomers to ask questions.

Facebook Group:
www.Facebook.com/groups/499248430155625/

This is an advanced group open by application for helping professionals who have had at least the Basic Introductory course.

BOOKS BY LAURIE WEISS

Emotional Self-Help: I Don't Need Therapy, but Where Do I Turn for Answers?

Answers to questions about ordinary life skills you rarely learn when you grow up in a dysfunctional home.

www.BooksByLaurie.com/answers

Recovery from CoDependency: It's Never Too Late to Reclaim Your Childhood

A map for therapists and Adult Children.

www.BooksByLaurie.com/recovery

An Action Plan for Your Inner Child: Parenting Each Other

For the times you feel like a child in a grown-up body, wishing for someone to take care of you.

http://tinyurl.com/hlc258c

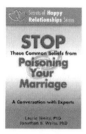

Stop These Common Beliefs from Poisoning Your Marriage. A Conversation with Experts.
Demystify the myths that may be undermining your marriage.
www.BooksByLaurie.com/stop

99 Things Women Wish They Knew Before... Saying "I Do."
Your guide to a successful and fulfilling marriage.
www.BooksByLaurie.com/99

Being Happy Together.
Create a fabulous relationship with your life partner in less than an hour a week.
www.BooksByLaurie.com/happy

What Is the Emperor Wearing? Truth-Telling in Business Relationships.
How to tell the truth and be appreciated instead of getting into trouble.
www.BooksByLaurie.com/emperor

36268869R00081

Made in the USA
Lexington, KY
12 April 2019

Release Your Anxiety and Stress in Minutes Starting NOW!

Everyone tells you to just let go of things that bother you—but you just can't figure out how!

Are you ready to learn a revolutionary new process to help you release that stress and anxiety in just a few minutes using only words?

- Stop worrying about things you can't control.
- Manage challenging situations.
- Stop imagining disasters.
- Turn off the thoughts that keep you awake at night.
- Transform your anxiety into relaxation.

Experience the freedom that comes from effortlessly managing previously distressing situations and even forget to worry about those things you used to obsess about.

This process has been called a tool, a form of prayer, and magical. Created by Swiss psychologist Dr. Willem Lammers, he calls it a guided self-change technique naming it Logosynthesis®. It's been used by psychotherapists and coaches since 2005 throughout Europe to help their clients eliminate stress, anxiety and worry.

Discover and use the three magic sentences to release your anxiety and toxic stress.Reclaim your life energy and the joy that is your birthright!

Letting It Go: Relieve Anxiety and Toxic Stress in Just a Few Minutes Using Only Words reveals how to easily learn to use this tool yourself, in private, to finally clarify and let go of those things that are draining your life energy.

"Laurie Weiss has taken the simplicity, elegance and effectiveness of Logosynthesis for self-coaching to new heights." DR. WILLEM LAMMERS, author of LOGOSYNTHESIS® Healing with Words

Dr. Laurie Weiss has a multifaceted background as an internationally known psychotherapist, executive and life coach, marriage counselor, relationship communication expert, trainer of professionals, speaker, grandmother and author of 7 books. Her current focus is on helping clients reclaim their life energy and find joy in all areas of their lives.

ISBN 9780974311357

90000 >

9 780974 311357